Managing Change

This workbook sets out to provide the practising manager with a practical approach to planning and managing significant changes. It will help the manager to determine the objectives, scope and direction of change and to formulate a structured implementation plan. Managers will learn to identify and measure the skills needed to handle change and to define activities that will develop those skills.

The workbook incorporates self-assessment exercises, company assessment exercises, and a new case study. Senior managers will be able to use the book to establish a well structured, co-ordinated and consistent project management approach to change. The workbook can also provide trainers with a vehicle for a management development programme designed to support major change.

Colin Carnall is Director of Graduate Studies at Henley, The Management College. He has fifteen years' experience as practitioner, management teacher and consultant in the field of managing change.

19

SELF-DEVELOPMENT FOR MANAGERS

A major new series of workbooks for managers, edited by Jane Cranwell-Ward at Henley, The Management College.

This series presents a selection of books, in workbook format, on a range of key management issues and skills. The books are designed to provide practising managers with the basis for self-development across a wide range of industries and occupations.

Topics to be covered in the series include: stress management; assertiveness training; effective problem solving; management of change; and team building. All the books in the series contain exercises and self-assessment material.

Each book will relate to other relevant books in the series, so that the series provides a coherent new approach to self-development for managers. Closely based on the latest management training initiatives, the books are designed to complement management development programmes, in-house company training, and management qualification programmes such as CMS, DMS, MBA and professional qualification programmes.

Jane Cranwell-Ward is the Director of Company Programmes at Henley, the Management College. She has extensive experience running management training programmes and stress management workshops, in both public and private sectors. She is the author of *Managing Stress*, published in 1986 by Pan.

Managing Change

Colin Carnall

London

First published 1991 by Routledge
11 New Fetter Lane, London EC4P 4EE

© 1991 Colin Carnall

Typeset by Leaper & Gard Ltd, Bristol
Printed and bound in Great Britain by
Biddles Ltd, Guildford and King's Lynn

British Library Cataloguing in Publication Data

Carnall, C.A. (Colin A.)
   Managing change.
   1. Organisational change. Management aspects
   I. Title   II. Series
   658.406

ISBN 0-415-04463-4

Contents

Figures and tables

FIGURES

TABLES

Preface

The effective management of change is a topic that concerns all managers from corporate headquarters to junior management. Today all managers must realize that change is going to be a constant feature of their working lives. Skills in being an effective change leader are at the core of the management competencies needed for the twenty-first century.

This book examines change at three levels. First, it explores change at the psychological level identifying the attitudes and skills needed to be an effective change leader. Second, it operates at the managerial level reviewing how managers can plan the change process to help ensure implementation without disasters and setback. Finally, there is the strategic level which shows how change must be managed as part of a coherent strategic plan.

The importance of this book became clear when a recent (absolutely true) case study was discussed relating to a major change of distribution systems in a pan-European company. Twenty-two national warehouses were closed on a night in July to be replaced by a single European warehouse. The change was an unmitigated disaster. Products were lost, systems collapsed, orders missed, expensive additional facilities had to be rented and the company became a laughing stock in the trade. How could this happen? The reason was that the change was handled in an amateurish way, and firing the European distribution director did little to repair the disaster.

If the distribution director and his team had managed the change utilizing the ideas, frameworks and checklists suggested in this book, I believe that the management disaster would have been avoided. Millions could have been saved and the inevitable stress and confusion which occurred could have been prevented.

Each book in this series presents skills and techniques needed by managers in the 1990s. The ability to manage change effectively is fundamental for a manager today, as are the related skills of problem solving and thriving on stress, the topics of two further books in the series.

Professor Colin Carnall has researched change management for many years and has gained a wealth of practical experience working with managers at Henley, The Management College, and offering consultancy advice to companies. He was therefore the ideal choice to write *Managing Change*.

Jane Cranwell-Ward
Series Editor

1 *Introduction*

We live in a period of accelerating change. Great political events change our perception of the world. Fundamental changes in society restructure our lives. New technology means that the impossible becomes commonplace. Change is all around us and the capacity to manage change effectively is the crucial attribute of a successful manager in today's organizations.

This book is about the techniques and skills which are needed to manage change with confidence, sensitivity and expertise. It is a workbook that asks you to participate and use ideas in relation to your own situation. Throughout the book you will find reference to a case study, 'Money Matters plc', which demonstrates how the techniques and ideas have been used in practice. You may find it useful to read the background to the case study (see Part II, p. 65) alongside the main text so that you can see how these techniques have been applied.

The book is aimed at three audiences. First, managers whose whole working life is concerned with managing change. Second, teachers and trainers who are committed to developing practical skills for all those who jobs require them to be change agents, and third, students of management whose future working life will be spent in facilitating useful change.

The workbook has been designed to help managers identify what needs to be changed to secure improved performance and effectiveness for their own organization. In addition it provides the opportunity to review personal management skills and the skills of the management team across a range of 'change management skills'. It is set out in two parts.

Part I of the workbook has been designed around a simple

framework of managing change as set out below. A number of techniques are included, each with guidance on how results can be analysed and interpreted.

Activity	Technique
	1 Corporate functional analysis
Organizational diagnosis	2 Organizational diagnosis questionnaire
	3 Improvement analysis
Implementing change	1 Implementation checklist 1
	2 Implementation checklist 2
Change managenent skills	1 Change management skills exercise
	2 Analysis of change management skills

Part II comprises an analysis of a financial services company, Money Matters plc, using the techniques set out in Part I. The case study sets out a diagnosis of the company, a discussion of the issues to be faced in managing changes in that business and concludes with an implementation plan. In Part I each technique is summarized by using information taken from the case study in Part II.

USING THE WORKBOOK

The workbook is designed to be used in a number of ways:

1   Any manager concerned to assess an organization carefully and systematically could complete the techniques creating

'personal action plans' for corporate and personal change and development.

2   The various questionnaires and checklists can be completed by groups of managers at management workshops/seminars. This can provide a more systematic basis for reviewing the organization, learning about how to manage change and identifying improvement and implementation plans for the future.

3   The questionnaires and checklists can be completed by either all or a sample of employees as input either to a management seminar/workshop dealing with the management of change or to individual/groups of managers responsible for planning and carrying out changes.

4   Managers may usefully select one or more of the techniques to help with either planning, implementing or monitoring the impact of change.

It is important to ensure that people are asked questions they can answer. Often, for example, the corporate functional analysis (see p. 16) is completed only by senior management. At the same time we should not ignore the individual's contribution, even if relevant to only a part of the analysis. Expectations are also important. Using techniques like these will create expectations. Therefore it makes sense to have worked out a strategy for dealing with the results before starting.

Whilst many readers will conclude that professional help would greatly assist the completion of data collection (e.g. use of questionnaires and interviews) and the interpretation of results, the workbook has been designed to assist people in organizations to *do it themselves.* Ultimately the successful use of these techniques should lead managers to think about problems and changes in new, more systematic and more effective ways. That is the objective of the author in producing this book.

Part I
The Workbook

2 Assessing organizational effectiveness

This exercise focuses on an internal analysis of the organization to identify its strengths and weaknesses. This will allow us to identify the organization's capabilities and resources, how well it is exploiting them, and how effectively it is adapting to changing environmental pressures. The exercise is in three parts:

1 Functional analysis
2 Organizational diagnosis
3 Organizational improvement analysis

FUNCTIONAL ANALYSIS

In this part of the workbook you should focus on the key functional elements of your organization, namely people, marketing, finance, operations/service and business/corporate development. Each section deals with one functional element and comprises a checklist of factors relating to that element. You are asked to assess the contribution to corporate objectives of each factor as a percentage. Record this figure in the *Score* column, and add your reasons for giving this score in the *Comments* column.

Factor 1.1, for example concerns the relationship between employees and the enterprise regarding pay. If groups of employees feel that the pay they receive is inadequate or if there is no clear link between improved performance and pay then we might conclude that corporate objectives are inadequately supported by the pay system. We would then enter a score of, say, 50% and record the main reasons for that score in comment form.

7

1 People issues

	Factor	*Score*	*Comments*
1.1	The design and operation of the pay system		
1.2	Promotion and career development opportunities		
1.3	Training and development		
1.4	The effectiveness of performance appraisal and review (whether a formal system or not)		
1.5	The skills and experience of employees		
1.6	The organization's policy regarding selection and placement of people		

	Factor	*Score*	*Comments*
1.7	The organization's relationship with trade unions represented within the enterprise		
1.8	The extent to which employees are motivated and encouraged to give their 'best' performance		
1.9	The quality of the information people have to do their job		
1.10	The extent to which human resources are considered when formulating and implementing strategic decisions		
People issues average			_____

2 Finance

	Factor	*Score*	*Comments*
2.1	The effectiveness of budget preparation		
2.2	The level of involvement of key staff in budget preparation		
2.3	The degree of consistency between divisional (unit) budgets and overall organizational budgets		
2.4	The degree of consistency between financial budgets and strategic plans		

Factor	Score	Comments
2.5 The effectiveness of management control		
2.6 The utilization of management information by managers		
2.7 The extent to which managers take corrective action to remedy problems		
2.8 The extent to which information from the management information system is used to achieve improved performance		
Finance average		

3 Marketing

Factor	*Score*	*Comments*
3.1 The contribution of each product/service group (or division, unit) to sales and profit. (You may wish to tackle this question separately for each group, division or unit)		
3.2 The market position of each product/ service group: market share growth maturity		

Factor	*Score*	*Comments*
3.3 The extent to which this organization competes effectively on: price quality service delivery		
3.4 The quality and extent of our knowledge of competitors		
3.5 The use of market research and its impact on product development		
Marketing average		_____

4 Operations/service

Factor	Score	Comments
4.1 The level of co-operation between marketing and operations/service departments		
4.2 The extent to which the information received from marketing, finance, etc. is useful for managing this function		
4.3 Management understanding of long run trends in: costs productivity resource utilization technology		
4.4 The extent to which management is able to control costs		

	Factor	*Score*	*Comments*
4.5	The level of inventory (raw material, work-in-progress, finished goods) in relation to output, sales and cash		
4.6	The adequacy, age and state of repair of plant, equipment and facilities		
4.7	The flexibility of use of plant, equipment and facilities		
4.8	The flexibility of staff		
4.9	The level of investment (compared to the average for the industry)		
4.10	The effectiveness of operations/planning		
Operations/service average			_____

5 Corporate/business development

	Factor	*Score*	*Comments*
5.1	The organization's investment in business development		
5.2	The ability of the organization to respond quickly to market and competitive pressures		
5.3	The organization's ability to exploit new products/services		
5.4	The extent to which the organization pursues opportunities for product/service improvement		
5.5	The integration of development with market, operations, finance, design, etc.		
5.6	The extent to which the organization is able to exploit outside sources for development purposes (e.g. joint ventures, universities, consultants)		
	Corporate/business development average	_____	

Analysis

For each of the five areas calculate the average score. Then subtract this average from each individual score to give a plus or minus percentage. Negative scores reveal weaknesses and positive scores strengths. Thus for each of the five areas, a list of strengths and weaknesses can be drawn up.

The next priority is to focus on the five functional areas as a whole. Any area where the average score is above 65 per cent may be considered as a strength. Areas with an average score of less than 65 per cent should then be examined. This cut-off is somewhat arbitrary – we are attempting to focus attention on priority areas where there is significant potential for improvement. We now have three lists.

1　Weaknesses

    a

    b

    c

    d

    e

2　Strengths

    a

    b

    c

    d

    e

3	Improvement priority
	a
	b
	c
	d
	e

MONEY MATTERS PLC

Set out below are the average 'scores' given by forty managers interviewed in the case study company, Money Matters plc (see Part II). The computation score minus the average score is given in brackets in the first column.

1 People issues

Factor	(Score−average score)	Score	Comments
1.1	(−12.5%)	40%	No incentives operate, base salaries are too low. An incentive scheme for managers was planned, announced and then not implemented.
1.2	(7.5%)	60%	Most particularly for graduate trainees, less so for locally-recruited staff but national systems open to all are in place.

Factor	(Score−average score)	Score	Comments
1.3	(−2.5%)	50%	Off-the-job training perceived to be excellent but not well organized. On-the-job training in bank systems is seen as poor.
1.4	(22.5%)	75%	Performance appraisal is well developed and seen to be effective.
1.5	(27.5%)	80%	Excellent but not fully utilized.
1.6	(12.5%)	65%	Good
1.7	(2.5%)	55%	Good
1.8	(−17.5%)	35%	The moves to achieve a 'sales culture', poor working conditions and non-competitive pay demotivate staff. Poor delegation is a key problem.
1.9	(−22.5%)	30%	Too much data, not enough information.
1.10	(−32.5%)	20%	Not perceived to be considered by top management who are regarded as 'exploiting the loyalty of their people'.
People issues average		**52.5%**	

Therefore for the people issues the strengths and weaknesses are:

Strengths	Weaknesses
Promotion/career development	Pay system
Performance appraisal	Training
Skills/experience of staff	Motivation
Selection and placement	Information
Company relations with trade unions	Planning

The average score is less than 65% therefore it rates as a priority area for improvement. Looking at the data more closely there is at least one apparent paradox. Career development/promotion is seen by these managers as a strength yet training and development is seen as a weakness. However, it is not anywhere near the highest scoring strength. The results are compatible because these managers see a nationally operated career development/promotion system which is well supported by the performance appraisal system. After many years of only limited training a very large amount of off-the-job training, dealing with leadership skills, managerial skills and selling skills, is underway. Unfortunately the extent of that training programme puts branches under pressure because not enough replacement staff are available. Moreover, managers and staff see on-the-job training in banking techniques as not being available at branch level. One staff member commented: 'It's become to be acceptable to make a mistake now'.

Motivation is seen as a key weakness partly because of the pay system and partly because of poor working conditions. There was also clear evidence of inadequate delegation to staff. This creates less satisfying work for staff which, in itself, is demotivating. Poor delegation often leads to delays in responding to customers, creating more customer complaints, which the staff are the first to handle. It also means that staff have less opportunity to develop on-the-job knowledge.

Clearly then, this short summary of part of the case study data suggests that significant improvements might be secured by examining management style, delegation and the way in which the work is arranged. Before going any further we should turn to the second technique.

ORGANIZATIONAL DIAGNOSIS

This questionnaire is designed to help you to determine how well your own organization works in a number of related areas.

Assess how far you agree or disagree with the following statements as they apply to you within your own department or section, using the seven-point scale and circling the appropriate number.

1	2	3	4	5	6	7
Agree Strongly	Agree	Agree Slightly	Neutral	Disagree Slightly	Disagree	Disagree Strongly

In answering the statements, try and be as honest as you can. This is not a test, and there are no right or wrong answers. The only correct answer is what you decide yourself.

Statement

1 I understand the objectives of this organization.
    1 2 3 4 5 6 7

2 The organization of work here is effective.
    1 2 3 4 5 6 7

3 Manager will always listen to ideas.
    1 2 3 4 5 6 7

4 I am encouraged to develop my full potential.
    1 2 3 4 5 6 7

5 My immediate boss has ideas that are helpful to me and my work group.
    1 2 3 4 5 6 7

6 My immediate boss is supportive and helps me in my work.
    1 2 3 4 5 6 7

7 This organization keeps its policies and procedures relevant and up to date.
    1 2 3 4 5 6 7

8 We regularly achieve our objectives.
    1 2 3 4 5 6 7

9   The goals and objectives   1   2   3   4   5   6   7
    of this organization are
    clearly stated.

10 Jobs and lines of authority   1   2   3   4   5   6   7
    are flexible.

11 I can always talk to   1   2   3   4   5   6   7
    someone at work if I have
    a work-related problem.

12 The salary that I receive is   1   2   3   4   5   6   7
    commensurate with the job
    that I perform.

13 I have all the information   1   2   3   4   5   6   7
    and resources I need to do
    a good job.

14 The management style   1   2   3   4   5   6   7
    adopted by senior
    management is helpful and
    effective.

15 We constantly review our   1   2   3   4   5   6   7
    methods and introduce
    improvements.

16 Results are attained   1   2   3   4   5   6   7
    because people are
    committed to them.

17 I feel motivated by the   1   2   3   4   5   6   7
    work I do.

18 The way in which work   1   2   3   4   5   6   7
    tasks are divided is sensible
    and clear.

19 My relationships with other   1   2   3   4   5   6   7
    members of my work
    group are good.

20 There are opportunities for   1   2   3   4   5   6   7
    promotion and increased
    responsibility in this
    organization.

21 This organization sets   1   2   3   4   5   6   7
    realistic plans.

22 Performance is regularly   1   2   3   4   5   6   7
    reviewed by my boss.

23 There are occasions when   1   2   3   4   5   6   7
    I would like to be free to
    make changes in my job.

24 People are cost conscious   1   2   3   4   5   6   7
    and seek to make the best
    use of resources.

25 The priorities of this   1   2   3   4   5   6   7
    organization are
    understood by its
    employees.

26 There is a constant search   1   2   3   4   5   6   7
    for ways of improving the
    way we work.

27 We co-operate effectively   1   2   3   4   5   6   7
    in order to get the work
    done.

28 Encouragement and   1   2   3   4   5   6   7
    recognition is given for all
    jobs and tasks in this
    organization.

29 Departments work well   1   2   3   4   5   6   7
    together to achieve good
    performance.

30 This organization's   1   2   3   4   5   6   7
    management team provides
    effective and inspiring
    leadership.

31 This organization has the capacity to change.   1 2 3 4 5 6 7

32 The work we do is always necessary and effective.   1 2 3 4 5 6 7

33 In my own work area objectives are clearly stated and each person's work role clearly identified.   1 2 3 4 5 6 7

34 The way the work structure in this organization is arranged produces general satisfaction.   1 2 3 4 5 6 7

35 Conflicts of views are resolved by solutions which are understood and accepted.   1 2 3 4 5 6 7

36 All individual work performance is reviewed against agreed standards.   1 2 3 4 5 6 7

37 Other departments are helpful to my own department whenever necessary.   1 2 3 4 5 6 7

38 My boss's management style helps me in the performance of my own work.   1 2 3 4 5 6 7

39 Creativity and initiative are encouraged.   1 2 3 4 5 6 7

40 People are always concerned to do a good job.   1 2 3 4 5 6 7

Analysis

Calculate the average score for all respondents on each statement. In analysing the data adopt the following three rules:

Rule 1

Any statement where more than 50 per cent of respondents score 3 or below is an identified strength for the organization.

Rule 2

Any statement where more than 50 per cent of respondents score 4 or more should be identified as an area of potential weakness for the organization. The neutral point is included because organizations in a changing and competitive world need high levels of effectiveness. Neutral responses suggest something less than that.

Rule 3

Any statement where more than 30 per cent score 5 or more should be identified as a weakness for the organization. It is worth noting that 10–15 per cent dissatisfaction is common in employee surveys. Whilst statements for which 10–15 per cent or more score 5 or above cannot be ignored, this rule adopts a cut-off well above that. Any weakness highlighted by Rule 3 is clearly something not to be ignored.

You now have three further lists.

1   Strengths

    a

    b

    c

    d

    e

2   Potential weaknesses

    a

    b

    c

    d

    e

3   Identified weaknesses

    a

    b

    c

    d

    e

MONEY MATTERS PLC

Listed below are the ten statements identified as potential weaknesses by applying Rules 2 and 3 to the case study questionnaire.

4 I am encouraged to develop my full potential.
12 The salary that I receive is commensurate with the job that I perform.
18 The way in which work tasks are divided is sensible and clear.
21 This organization sets realistic plans.
28 Encouragement and recognition is given for all jobs and tasks in this organization.
30 This organization's management team provides effective and inspiring leadership.
32 The work we do is always necessary and effective.
34 The way the work structure in this organization is arranged produces general satisfaction.
35 Conflicts of views are resolved by solutions which are understood and accepted.
38 My boss's management style helps me in the performance of my own work.

Two more statements emerge as weaknesses from Rule 2:

13 I have all the information and resources I need to do a good job.
17 I feel motivated by the work I do.

This powerfully supports and extends the functional analysis (see pp. 7–18). Evidently management style, support and the organization of work are key areas. Responses to questions 12, 18, 32, 34 and 17 indicate that staff do not feel the work is effectively structured, always necessary and motivating. Responses to questions 4, 28, 30, 35 and 38 suggest that staff perceive a lack of encouragement, recognition, help, leadership and satisfactory decision making from management. Could it be that the unwillingness of managers to delegate tasks to staff puts the managers under pressure – too much pressure to allow them enough time to work with staff – and demotivates staff as well? Could it be that the lack of training – historically and more recently regarding on-the-job training – is

one of the reasons why managers do not delegate? Does this reinforce a risk-averse culture in which risk taking, creativity and inno-
vation are discouraged?

The responses to questions 21 and 13 suggest that staff do not
perceive realistic plans nor do they feel adequately informed or
resourced. Do they see the company's future plans as being credible? What does that suggest for the prospects of implementation
of changes such as the move toward a sales culture?

Now proceed to the next technique.

ORGANIZATIONAL IMPROVEMENT ANALYSIS

For this technique you should try to identify ways of improving
your organization to deal with the weaknesses you have already
identified. Now complete the following questionnaire.

---

1   What are the main strengths of your department?

a

b

c

d

e

2   What are the most important areas in which your department's performance could be improved?

a

b

c

d

e

---

3   List practical ways in which your department's performance might be improved

a

b

c

d

e

4   How might your department improve the quality of its
output/the service it provides its customers/clients?

a

b

c

d

e

5   Do you think you are given, or have access to, enough
information to do your job effectively? Please tick the
appropriate box.

Yes ☐ Most of the time ☐ Some of the time ☐ No ☐

6   How might the quality of information available to you be
improved?

a

b

c

d

e

Analysis

You now combine the results of all three parts.

Corporate functional analysis

Strengths

a

b

c

d

e

Organizational diagnosis

Strengths

a

b

c

d

e

Improvement analysis

Strengths (question 1)

a

b

c

d

e

Blockages (question 2)

a

b

c

d

e

Improvement priorities (from functinal analysis)

a

b

c

d

e

Weaknesses (from functional analysis)

a

b

c

d

e

Potential weaknesses (from organizational diagnosis)

a

b

c

d

e

Identified weaknesses (from organizatinal diagnosis)

a

b

c

d

e

Practical steps for improvement (questions 3, 4 and 6)

a

b

c

d

e

f

g

h

Analysis

Identify how the improvement ideas listed could meet the problems identified through the weaknesses. In particular focus on how strengths can be utilized to deal with blockages to improvement. List possible action steps

1

2

3

4

5

6

MONEY MATTERS PLC

An example of this analysis is now given for Money Matters plc. Listed below are the blockages to improvement identified by both managers and staff in the company.

- Facilities: inadequate both operationally and in terms of customer service and image; inadequate computer systems
- Training: inadequate training in bank systems and procedures; lack of experienced staff at branch level
- Work Pressure: understaffed; too much pressure
- Ineffective management: no leadership; poor attitudes from some managers; inefficient organization of work; too much bureaucracy
- Information: too much paper; not enough information

The strengths identified by managers or staff are:

- Loyalty and experience of staff
- Team spirit at branch level
- Product range
- The area management team
- Open management style
- Customer base
- Growth in the local economy

Can any of these strengths be utilized in working with the blockages? The existing customer base in a fast-growing local economy suggests that a good platform for change exists. On management/leadership the evidence suggests that the relatively recently established area management team is seen as a strength – there are doubts about management focusing on the middle levels of the company, particularly at branch level. All staff are seen as loyal. Many are also very experienced. The point raised about lack of experience relates to younger staff who are seen as not receiving anything approaching adequate training.

These factors, considered with the earlier discussion of delegation and work organization, make it clear that one way forward would be to increase the utilization of the skills/experience of senior staff at branch level. Interestingly significant numbers of branch managers would ultimately welcome the opportunity to free themselves from some routine work to allow more time for business development. In turn this requires attention to the risk averse culture. Again it is interesting to note that the bank's national policy of having freely available information may reinforce this culture. All managers receive all circulars, instructions, papers and so on. The bulk of information is impressive. One day's package can run to three or four inches! But once you have had it, beware of making a mistake. At area level branch managers are called in to fortnightly performance review meetings. These last all day. The area team goes through the performance data, which is printed off the computer, branch by branch. All branch managers sit through the whole meeting. Many report it as time wasting and boring. It adds to the pressure but not to business development.

It has now been agreed that the performance review shall only take part of the day and be presented in summary form. Particular problems or successes can be discussed at an individual level. The rest of the meeting will focus on a key current issue and will take a workshop approach. The rule will be that if we call the managers in together we wish them to work on a relevant problem. Everyone should perceive value from the time expended. In essence the changes are about structuring the use of time and shifting from performance review as a 'search for the guilty' towards a more problem-focused approach. It will take time but given the quality of the area management team and its perceived open management style, slow but steady progress can be expected.

Thus some *action steps* would be:

■ Structure the performance review meetings more effectively (area management team).
■ Provide more product and systems training at branch level (branch managers/senior staff supported by training manager).
■ Involve senior branch staff in reviewing work methods/organization at branch level.

(See Part II, p. 86 for the complete list.)

You have now seen how to develop a fairly systematic diagnosis of what needs to be changed, identifying priorities and working towards action plans. The next step is to manage the implementation of change.

Now turn to the implementation exercise.

3 The Implementation Exercise

This exercise comprises two checklists. The checklists are designed to help you think about aspects of the organization which might help or hinder the implementation of change. Please complete the two checklists by focusing on a significant organizational change in which you have been or are now involved. Fill in details of the change below before turning to the checklist.

Objectives

Scope and type of change (e.g. reorganization, new product, new technology)

Who is affected and how

Timetable for implementation

CHECKLIST 1: READINESS FOR CHANGE

Please tick the appropriate statement

1   In the past new policies or systems introduced by management have been: Seen as meeting employees' needs ☐

2   Employees may be best described as: Innovative ☐

3   The most recent and widely known change in the organization is viewed as: A success ☐

4   Expectations of what change will lead to are: Consistent throughout the organization ☐

5   What can people directly affected by the changes tell you about the organization's business or strategic plan?   A full description   ☐

6   Outcomes of the change have been: Specified in detail ☐

7   Present work procedures to be affected by the change are seen as needing: Major change ☐

8   The problems to be dealt with by the changes were first raised by: The people directly involved ☐

9   The proposed change is viewed by end users as: Crucial to the organization's future ☐

10   Top management support for the proposed change is: Enthusiastic ☐

11   Top management has: Committed significant resources to the change ☐

12   The management performance appraisal and review process is: An important part of management development ☐

13   The proposed change deals with issues of relevance to the business plan: Directly ☐

14   The proposed change: Makes jobs more rewarding financially and otherwise ☐

15   The proposed change is technically: Similar to others already under way ☐

Not well understood ☐	Greeted with some resistance ☐	Vigorously resisted ☐
Independent ☐	Apathetic ☐	Conservative or resistant to change ☐
Moderately successful ☐	Had no obvious impact ☐	Not successful ☐
Consistent amongst senior management but not otherwise ☐	Not at all consistent ☐	Unclear ☐
A description of where it affects their own department or activity ☐	A general idea ☐	Nothing ☐
Outlined in general terms ☐	Poorly defined ☐	Not defined ☐
Significant alteration ☐	Minor improvement ☐	No change ☐
First-line management and supervision ☐	Senior management ☐	Outside consultants ☐
Generally beneficial to the organization ☐	Beneficial only to part of the organization ☐	Largely a matter of procedure ☐
Limited ☐	Minimal ☐	Unclear ☐
Expects the change to be implemented from existing resources ☐	Has withheld resources ☐	Has not planned the resources needed ☐
A helpful problem solving process ☐	Routine ☐	An obstacle to improvement ☐
Partly ☐	Only indirectly ☐	Not at all ☐
Makes jobs easier and more satisfying ☐	Replaces old tasks and skills with new ones ☐	Makes jobs harder ☐
Similar to others undertaken in the recent past ☐	Novel ☐	Unclear technically ☐

CHECKLIST 2: MANAGING CHANGE

Please tick the appropriate statement.

1	The implementation plan provides:	Clear targets ☐
2	The likelihood of project deadlines being met is:	High ☐
3	Day-to-day control of implementation is being managed by:	One specific person ☐
4	Implementation begins in:	One small work area or department ☐
5	The plan is being introduced:	Almost 'over-night' ☐
6	Those involved initially were selected:	Because they were flexible and supportive ☐
7	Training is being carried forward with:	Outside training only ☐
8	Training is designed to:	Solve problems with the new system ☐
9	Training involves:	Only key end users or those affected ☐
10	Implementation of the change will:	Allow people full control of the tasks they perform ☐
11	Managers discuss changes with users and others:	To develop the plans for change ☐
12	Implementation has:	Built-in incentives and rewards ☐
13	Benefits will occur:	Immediately ☐
14	Direct benefits will be:	Clearly apparent to users ☐
15	Effects will be:	Measurable in quantitative terms ☐
16	During change people need to put in:	Very considerable effort, skill and extra work ☐
17	Management provides people with:	Excellent support ☐
18	People experience:	High levels of pressure or stress during change ☐

Acceptable targets □	Broad objectives □	No targets □
Moderate □	Low □	Non-existent □
Several people □	No one specific individual □	Not sure □
A number of units □	A major department or division □	Throughout the organization □
Rapidly □	Gradually □	Very slowly □
Because they were very committed to the organization □	Because they most needed the change □	No reason □
Specially designed sessions in-house plus outside training □	Technical or user manuals □	Not at all □
Involve the user's experience □	Designed for a wide range of audiences □	Takes no account of users □
Involves everyone affected □	Does not involve end users □	No training provided □
Help people better control the tasks they do □	Mean that tasks are controlled by the 'system' or the technology □	Control the people performing the tasks □
To get ideas and feedback on implementation □	To keep them informed □	To control progress □
Provision for some recognition of success □	No specific incentives □	Problems for the people using the system □
Quickly □	Within a year of implementation □	Over a year following implementation □
Apparent only to managers □	Apparent only to top managers □	Only indirect benefits □
Measurable only as 'ratings' □	Largely anecdotal □	Not clear □
Considerable effort, skill and extra work □	Some extra effort, skill and work □	No extra effort, skill or work □
Good support □	Limited support □	No support □
Considerable pressure or stress during change □	Some pressure or stress during change □	No stress during change □

The two checklists deal with a range of implementation problems. Set out below is a summary of the techniques and principles which can be applied to alleviate these implementation problems. Each box lists questions related to a set of three points in one of the two checklists. If you tended to select the third or fourth option for completing a statement in any group of three points, then it would be worth reviewing the relevant techniques for your own organization.

METHODS FOR IMPLEMENTING CHANGE

Checklist 1: readiness for change

To deal with resistance to change (points 1–3)

> Has there been unsuccessful past experience of change?
> Do we have a risk-averse culture?
> Are there communication problems?

Keep everyone informed by making information available; explaining plans clearly; allowing access to management for questions and clarification.

Ensure that change is sold realistically by making a practical case for change; explain change in terms which the employee will see as relevant and acceptable; show how change fits business needs and plans; spend time and effort on presentations.

Prepare carefully by making a full organizational diagnosis; spend time with people and groups, building trust, understanding and support.

Involve people by getting feedback on proposals; get people to fill out the checklists; discuss the data from these checklists.

Start small and successfully by piloting a receptive group of employees, and in departments with a successful track record; implement changes in clear phases.

Plan for success by starting with changes that can give a quick and positive pay-off; publicize early success; provide positive feedback to those involved in success.

To clarify the effects of change (points 4–6)

What are people's expectations of change?
What are the objectives of change?

Clarify benefits of changes by emphasizing benefits to those involved and to the company.

Emphasize where the new systems utilize existing knowledge and skills.

Minimize surprises by specifying all assumptions about the change; focus on outcomes; identify potential problems.

Communicate plans by being specific in terms familiar to the different groups of employees; communicate periodically and through various media; ask for feedback; do not suppress negative views but listen to them carefully and deal with them openly.

To identify *ownership* of change (points 7–9)

Are procedures, systems, departments, products and services seen as a problem?
Who planned the changes – top management or a staff department?

Plan for visible outcomes from change.

Clarify employees' views by exploring their concerns about the changes and examining impact on the day-to-day routines.

Specify who wants change and why; explain longer term advantages; identify common benefits; present potential of change.

To ensure top management support (points 10–12)

> Will top management support the changes openly?
> Will top management provide the necessary resources?
> Is the management performance appraisal process an
>   obstacle to change?

Build a power base by becoming the expert in the problems involved; understand top management concerns; develop information and formal support; develop a strong and polished presentation in top management language.

Develop clear objectives and plans by establishing a clear timetable; set up review processes to be supportive, involving top management and middle management; focus meetings on specific outcomes and specific problems.

To create acceptance of changes (points 13–15)

> Do the planned changes fit other business plans?
> Is there a clear sense of direction?
> Do the proposed changes place greater demands on people?
> Does the change involve new technology or expertise?

Identify relevance of change to plans by reviewing plans and specifying how change fits; incorporate changes into on-going developments; if possible, frame changes in terms of the organization's style.

Implement changes using flexible or adaptable people, who are familiar with some or all of the change; in a part of the business where there are strong supporters for change; recognize why people support change (career, rewards, company politics).

Do not oversell change. Be clear about conflicts with present practices; encourage discussion of these conflicts.

To build an effective team to implement change (points 16–18)

> Will team members be inflexible in dealing with change?
> Will managers need to work hard to ensure commitment
> to changes.

Ensure that teams have clear and agreed goals.

Involve all members of the team in ways they each see as relevant and using their own skills/expertise.

Be prepared to face and deal with conflict.

Encourage constructive feedback.

Checklist 2: managing change

To clarify plans for change (points 1–3)

> Do we have clear plans, deadlines and milestones?
> Is there clear accountability?
> Do we have a realistic timetable?

Assign one person to be accountable overall for change and ensure clear accountability at all levels.

Define goals carefully by checking feasibility with people involved, experts, other companies; use measurable goals where possible but always looking at broader goals and outcomes.

Define specific goals by defining small, clear steps, identifying and publicizing critical milestones; assign firm deadlines.

Translate plans into action by publishing plans; build in rewards for performance; give regular feedback.

To build new systems and practices into the organization (points 4–6)

> How wide is the scope/scale of change?
> Are people supportive, informed, prepared?

Plan the rate of change carefully by piloting to learn from experience; implement for success, small steps and specific milestones; allow *more* time.

Enlist firm support; ensure that new procedures, products and services are well understood.

To provide training and support (points 7–9)

> Are we providing specific, relevant training?
> Is the training flexible and geared to people's needs?
> Is the training supported in the work place?
> Are we targeting the right people for training?

Clarify objectives of training; use existing skills and knowledge; depend on people as part of implementation; use suggestions as part of the training.

Allow people to learn at their own pace; provide opportunities for hands-on experience; make training relevant to the job; have line managers project manage training.

Use different learning approaches; respect and use people's experience; allow people to solve problems and utilize their solutions.

Incorporate feedback into training programme.

To build commitment to change (points 10–12)

> Does the change impose new controls on people,
>   performances, costs, etc?
> Does the change reduce discretion?
> Are there incentives built into the change?

Plan change to bring benefits by using it to increase personal control over the job (and accountability); enhance people's jobs and status; ensure quick, visible benefits; provide incentives for people to go for change.

Involve people by asking for suggestions; specify milestones and ask for feedback; publicize ways in which suggestions and feedback are utilized.

To provide feedback to those involved (points 13–15)

> Do visible benefits occur?
> Is the impact on cost, performance, profit, resource
>   utilization, etc. well documented?

Make sure that results are well documented, accessible, quickly available, positively described, relevant; ensure achievement of milestones is recognized.

Arrange wide recognition of success of people involved throughout the organization; specify how the change has helped the organization achieve its goals.

To manage the stress induced by change (points 16–18)

> Are people subject to high levels of stress?
> Is performance declining due to stress?
> Is there a higher incidence of 'people' problems?

Plan change to control the impact on people; seek ways of controlling the pressure.

Allow more resources and time where the changes are novel.

Adopt a rapid implementation plan where people have been consulted and agree to change.

Empathy – constantly reinforce change – communicate and listen.

MONEY MATTERS PLC

From the implementation exercise one aspect of implementation at Money Matters plc which emerged as needing particular attention was the problem of resistance to change. Two management workshops were set up to consider the implementation of change at Money Matters. Thirty-two participants responded to points 1–3 of Checklist 1 in the following percentages.

Please tick the appropriate statement.

		Seen as meeting employees' needs	Not well understood	Greeted with some resistance	Vigorously resisted
1	In the past, new policies or systems introduced by management have been:	5%	18%	56%	21%
		Innovative	Independent	Apathetic	Conservative or resistant to change
2	Employees may be best described as:	0%	32%	45%	23%
		A success	Moderately successful	Had no obvious impact	Not successful
3	The most recent and widely known change in the organization is viewed as:	0%	15%	56%	29%

We know from the organizational assessment and from the above that the bank culture is risk-averse. The statements selected for these three points at Money Matters plc were predominantly the third or fourth options. Possible techniques for dealing with resistance to change and risk aversion are listed on p. 40. Therefore in developing an implementation plan for Money Matters plc we should consider ways of building into the plan:

- clear and accessible information for employees
- that changes are sold realistically with benefits clearly described
- that managers spend time diagnosing problems carefully
- that changes are started with pilot schemes
- that pilot schemes are introduced such that early success can be obtained

4 Change management skills

Gaining an understanding of an individual's change management skills provides a good basis for individual development. This exercise comprises a questionnaire on change management skills. These skills have been identified from research into a wide range of management jobs across a range of change management settings and situations.

Complete Part A of the questionnaire by rating the importance of the skill now and in the future (for example in five years' time) by using the five-point scale and circling the appropriate number. In some cases, therefore, you will have two ratings, for example:

		Now		Future
1.1 Identifies problems and causes systematically	1 2	③	4	⑤

You should complete one copy of the questionnaire, and ideally a second copy should be completed by your manager.

Complete Part B of the questionnaire by rating your own performance in terms of each skill listed. Please leave some time between completing Part A and Part B.

PART A: IMPORTANCE OF SKILL

1	2	3	4	5
Not important	Of some importance	Important but not essential	Definitely of importance	Of vital importance

1 Preparing for change

1.1	Identifies problems and causes systematically	1	2	3	4	5
1.2	Remains calm under pressure	1	2	3	4	5
1.3	Involves others when appropriate	1	2	3	4	5
1.4	Builds an open climate for decision making	1	2	3	4	5
1.5	Sets and agrees objectives	1	2	3	4	5
1.5	Draws out the input and contribution of others	1	2	3	4	5
1.7	Checks for agreement to proposals	1	2	3	4	5
1.8	Reviews objectives carefully	1	2	3	4	5
1.9	Seeks all information relevant to a decision	1	2	3	4	5
1.10	Is effective in presenting ideas and proposals	1	2	3	4	5

2 Planning changes

2.1	Identifies opportunities and solutions	1	2	3	4	5
2.2	Evaluates options critically	1	2	3	4	5
2.3	Communicates information and views clearly	1	2	3	4	5
2.4	Generates imaginative solutions to problems	1	2	3	4	5
2.5	Identifies problems of implementation, resources required and appropriate priorities	1	2	3	4	5

3 Implementing changes

3.1	Identifies what needs to be done to achieve a plan for change	1	2	3	4	5
3.2	Achieves deadlines and meets appropriate priorities	1	2	3	4	5
3.3	Identifies impact of changes on people	1	2	3	4	5
3.4	Identifies and deals with impact of pressure/stress on self	1	2	3	4	5
3.5	Identifies and deals with impact of pressure/stress on others	1	2	3	4	5
3.6	Allocates tasks sensibly	1	2	3	4	5
3.7	Co-ordinates plans and actions effectively	1	2	3	4	5

4 Sustaining changes

4.1	Makes the time to review progress and problems	1	2	3	4	5
4.2	Discusses problems and issues openly	1	2	3	4	5
4.3	Provides relevant positive feedback to people	1	2	3	4	5
4.4	Identifies areas for improvement	1	2	3	4	5
4.5	Builds well on success, keeping motivation high	1	2	3	4	5
4.6	Builds team spirit	1	2	3	4	5
4.7	Sets out to increase the use of resources	1	2	3	4	5
4.8	Allows enough time for change	1	2	3	4	5

PART B: INDIVIDUAL'S PERFORMANCE

1	2	3	4		5
Inadequate	Poor	Average	Very good		Excellent

1 Preparing for change

1.1	Identifies problems and causes systematically	1	2	3	4	5
1.2	Remains calm under pressure	1	2	3	4	5
1.3	Involves others when appropriate	1	2	3	4	5
1.4	Builds an open climate for decision making	1	2	3	4	5
1.5	Sets and agrees objectives	1	2	3	4	5
1.6	Draws out the input and contribution of others	1	2	3	4	5
1.7	Checks for agreement to proposals	1	2	3	4	5
1.8	Reviews objectives carefully	1	2	3	4	5
1.9	Seeks all information relevant to a decision	1	2	3	4	5
1.10	Is effective in presenting ideas and proposals	1	2	3	4	5

2 Planning changes

2.1	Identifies opportunities and solutions	1	2	3	4	5
2.2	Evaluates options critically	1	2	3	4	5
2.3	Communicates information and views clearly	1	2	3	4	5
2.4	Generates imaginative solutions to problems	1	2	3	4	5
2.5	Identifies problems of implementation, resources required and appropriate priorities	1	2	3	4	5

3 Implementing changes

3.1   Identifies what needs to be done   1   2   3   4   5
      to achieve a plan for change

3.2   Achieves deadlines and meets   1   2   3   4   5
      appropriate priorities

3.3   Identifies impact of changes on   1   2   3   4   5
      people

3.4   Identifies and deals with impact   1   2   3   4   5
      of pressure/stress on self

3.5   Identifies and deals with impact   1   2   3   4   5
      of pressure/stress on others

3.6   Allocates tasks sensibly   1   2   3   4   5

3.7   Co-ordinates plans and actions   1   2   3   4   5
      effectively

4 Sustaining changes

4.1   Makes the time to review progress   1   2   3   4   5
      and problems

4.2   Discusses problems and issues   1   2   3   4   5
      openly

4.3   Provides relevant positive   1   2   3   4   5
      feedback to people

4.4   Identifies areas for improvement   1   2   3   4   5

4.5   Builds well on success, keeping   1   2   3   4   5
      motivation high

4.6   Builds team spirit   1   2   3   4   5

4.7   Sets out to increase the use of   1   2   3   4   5
      resources

4.8   Allows enough time for change   1   2   3   4   5

Analysis

Now enter your scores from the questionnaire.

	Part A Importance now	Part A Future importance	Part B Performance
1.1			
1.2			
1.3			
1.4			
1.5			
1.6			
1.7			
1.8			
1.9			
1.10			
2.1			
2.2			
2.3			
2.4			
2.5			
3.1			
3.2			
3.3			
3.4			
3.5			
3.6			
3.7			
4.1			
4.2			
4.3			
4.4			
4.5			
4.6			
4.7			
4.8			

If both you and your manager have completed the questionnaires you can now identify your strengths, skill development needs and change management development needs.

Strengths Those rated 4 or 5 on your performance by both you and your manager.

Skill development needs Those rated important *now* (3, 4 or 5) by you *and* your manager, but where your performance is inadequate (2 or 1) as rated by you *or* your manager.

Change management development needs Those rated by your manager as likely to be important (4 or 5) in 3–5 years' time but where your performance is inadequate (2 or 1) as rated by you *or* your manager.

Strengths

a

b

c

d

e

Skills development needs

a

b

c

d

e

Action (list possible actions to meet skills development needs)

a

b

c

d

e

f

Change management development needs

a

b

c

d

e

Action (list possible actions to meet change management development needs)

a

b

c

d

e

MONEY MATTERS PLC

From this exercise a key weakness identified for Money Matters plc was in the area of feedback-sustaining change. The feedback processes were too formal, too structured and one way. One of the changes included in the implementation plan was designed to create a more open and problem-orientated approach to performance review meetings. The present approach tended to leave managers, particularly branch managers, feeling very defensive about performance issues. This mitigated against open discussions of problems and reinforced the risk-averse culture. Drawing these managers into the discussion of 'group' problems at review meetings is one way of working with this weakness by changing the way the review meetings are handled. In consequence the manager running the performance review meeting needs to develop higher-level presentation skills, team-building skills and feedback skills. These are skills development needs. Possible actions to meet these needs include attending a presentation skills course, and restructuring the performance review meetings by interspersing shorter presentations with problem-solving sessions where groups of managers work on problems identified in the presentation. The presentations skills course will improve the level of skills, shorter presentations are likely to be more focused and draw a better audience response, and problem solving involves people, builds teams and presents opportunities for feedback.

A change management development need identified was that of motivating the sales force. Managers in the group understood how to motivate branch staff but not sales staff. This is a major development area for managers.

5 Project management of change

There is good reason to believe that significant changes would benefit from a 'project management' approach. Sometimes a manager is selected to concentrate full time on managing a major change. Sometimes a management steering group is established to oversee change. Often steering groups are established with a senior manager devoted full time or part time to the implementation of change. Such measures can only be justified where the scope and importance of the changes is of real significance to the organization. Where that is the case a project management approach can bring significant added value to implementation.

Changes require careful planning and sensitive implementation. In Tables 5.1 and 5.2 we list the pitfalls and problems identified in a survey of corporate planning (Table 5.1) and a survey of strategy implementation (Table 5.2). Evidently typical pitfalls in corporate planning are to do with lack of top-line management involvement; lack of clear goals; lack of flexibility in planning, and a failure to monitor and review performance against plans using the targets set as standards. That top management consistently short-circuits plans should surprise no one: the other pitfalls listed above suggest that it often sees plans as both remote and inflexible.

Table 5.1 The ten major traps in corporate planning (sample: 215 firms)

1   Top management's assumption that it can delegate the planning function to a planner.

2   Top management becomes so engrossed in current problems that it spends insufficient time on long-range planning and the process becomes discredited among other managers and staff.

3   Failure to develop company goals which are suitable as a basis for formulating long-range plans.

4   Failure to obtain the necessary involvement of major line personnel in the planning process.

5   Failure to use the plan as a standard for measuring managerial performance.

6   Failure to create a climate in the company which is congenial and not resistant to planning.

7   Assuming that corporate comprehensive planning is something separate from the entire management process.

8   Injecting so much formality into the system that it lacks flexibility, looseness and simplicity, and restrains creativity.

9   Failure of top management to review with departmental and divisional heads the long-range plans which they have developed.

10 Top management consistently rejects the formal planning mechanism by making intuitive decisions which conflict with formal plans.

As shown in Table 5.2, strategy implementation problems include inadequate time scale; unforeseen contingencies and problems over priorities; insufficient definition of implementation tasks; and inadequate monitoring of progress. These might be summarized as inadequate planning leading to inflexible plans of insufficient detail, i.e. the 'worst of both worlds'. A lack of top management leadership and support, insufficient attention to monitoring progress and inadequate training and support for employees involved also feature as problems. Interestingly lack of resources does not emerge. This is consistent with a 1986 MORI survey which dealt with problems of implementing change. Only a minority of the managers surveyed reported lack of resources as a problem of change implementation.

Table 5.2 The ten most frequent strategy implementation problems
(sample: 93 firms)

	Problem	Percentage of firms
1	Implementation took more time than originally allocated.	76
2	Major problems surfaced during implementation which had not been identified beforehand.	74
3	Coordination of implementation activities was not effective enough.	66
4	Competing activities and crises distracted management from implementing the decision.	64
5	Capabilities of employees involved were not sufficient.	63
6	Training and instruction given to lower-level employees was inadequate.	62
7	Uncontrollable factors in the external environment had an adverse impact on implementation.	60
8	Leadership and direction provided by department managers were not effective.	59
9	Key implementation tasks and activities were not defined in sufficient detail.	56
10	Information systems used to monitor implementation were inadequate.	56

In Table 5.3 we set out an outline of a project management strategy for managing change. For each element of the strategy we identify the 'added value' the element would offer as part of a change management strategy. We then list those problems which would need to be managed in order to utilize the element as a part of your strategy and identify those problems which are avoidable. The latter are problems which can be avoided altogether by careful use of the element. For example, if there is inadequate involvement of people in the process of change, poor communication and inadequate training and support, establishing a clear management structure to manage change will only serve to reduce motivation and commitment. There will necessarily be less personal accountability but a well organized and defined structure may well ensure clearer and more comprehensive, and therefore, more acceptable accountabilities.

Table 5.3 A project management strategy for managing change

Strategy	Added value	Key problems	Avoidable problems
1 Establish a management structure to implement change			
Management steering group	Wide discussion of issues	Less personal accountability	May reduce motivation commitment and ownership
Project manager	Involvement		
Working parties	Synergy		
Attitude surveys of staff	Input of professional expertise		
Management consultants	Learn from others' experience		

Strategy	Added value	Key problems	Avoidable problems

2 More extensive planning for implementation of change

Strategy	Added value	Key problems	Avoidable problems
Targets and milestones	Thorough search for best strategies	Reduced freedom of action	Plans may be inflexible
Resources required	Greater certainty for those involved	Confidentiality	
Timing of change	Priorities/ resources planned for	Slower decisions	
Identifying impact on people and preparing training, grading, counselling, and other measures	Sense of direction		

3 Effective leadership at all levels

Strategy	Added value	Key problems	Avoidable problems
Personal accountability	Bolder approaches possible	Has 'ownership' connotations	Interference
Teambuilding	Shared purposes	Objectivity of top management?	Over-ambitious strategies for change
Vision	Commitment		Too rapid an implementation plan
Communication			

Table 5.3 (continued)

Strategy	Added value	Key problems	Avoidable problems

4 Use long-term criteria in change planning and implementation

Focus on future requirements	Sense of vision and shared purpose	Less clear targets and accountability	Over optimism
Develop skills and technology	Builds credibility	Slower reactions in difficult product-market conditions	
Build adaptability	Share in success		

5 Flexible controls

| Focus on solutions to problems | Encourages innovation, risk-taking | Subjective assessments | Corporate politics |
| Recognize success | Allows more determined pursuit of long-term goals | Less accountability | |

6 Communications plan

Regular and repeated communications	Allows for adjustment of plans in the light of experience	Confidentiality issue	
Multi-media	Avoids misunderstanding	Timing of announcements	Rumour
Feedback, two-way	Builds recognition of goals and plans		
	Builds commitment		

MONEY MATTERS PLC

In Money Matters plc the group management team have accepted responsibility for implementing changes. All managers and staff have been interviewed or have responded to a survey. Staff meetings have been held. The group manager has presented the findings and the implementation plan to managers and staff. All of this sets out a management structure for implementation which managers and staff can understand. The implementation plan provides for training, stress counselling, sets targets and milestones and deals with timing issues. Much of the content of the changes being implemented focuses on teambuilding and more effective communication. The implementation plan identifies clear accountabilities. The changes will be monitored as part of the developing performance review process. The need to recognize success in a concrete fashion is built into the plan as is a two-way feedback. In many respects, therefore, the implementation plan meets the requirements identified in the project management strategy for change outlined in Table 5.3. This approach is designed to deal with any pitfalls and problems and follows on from the implementation exercise. You should now turn to Part II of this workbook to examine more fully the case study of Money Matters plc, an organization experiencing major changes.

Part II
The Case Study

6 *Money Matters plc*

INTRODUCTION

This workbook was used as the basis for a review of a regional group within Money Matters plc. Money Matters is a UK clearing bank offering a wide range of banking services to personal and corporate customers. Nationally the company is divided into twelve regions. Each region is divided into a number of groups and each group comprises up to twenty branch offices and other departments. Money Matters has only recently established the group structure, which is outlined in Figure 6.1.

Figure 6.1 The group structure of Money Matters plc

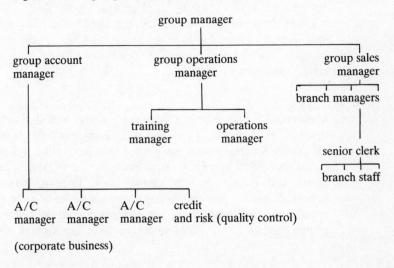

The group chosen for review is responsible for personal accounts and small/medium-sized corporate accounts (facilities up to £500,000). Money Matters has a separate corporate division for large corporate business. All managers in the chosen group were interviewed and a questionnaire was sent to all staff. At the time of the study various changes were either underway or expected/projected as follows:

- Significant development in technology including a switch to centralized processing of personal account transactions (cheques, transfers, etc.).
- Rebuilding and branch refurbishment (an extensive programme is underway in the group).
- The development of a performance-related pay system linked to sales performances.
- Attempts to shift Money Matters to a sales culture.

For simplicity the information presented below is restricted to that obtained from a detailed review of one group (we will call it the Midvale Group). Four groups, representative of the region as a whole, have been studied.

MANAGEMENT VIEWS

Set out below is a summary and analysis of the forty interviews conducted within the Midvale Group. Before the interview these managers had completed the organizational assessment set out in Chapter 2 of the workbook. The interviews allowed the author to clarify their views.

Job definition

Managers felt that their jobs were increasingly well-defined, partly through the evolution of the 'group concept', partly because of the job profile system, a well-established job description system used by Money Matters. There was evidence of flexibility between group and branch level responsibilities. Overall, however, it appeared that the present structure was not believed to be entirely conducive to Money Matters' emerging sales culture. The level and responsibilities of the sales manager were questioned. Was the level too low? Were the authorities of branch managers sufficient? Were all the branch managers adapting to their new responsibilities? The group concept was recognized as a significant organizational change, placing demands on the staff, for whom training, on-the-job experience and the process of appraisal and review are only slowly providing support. Important in all of this were the level of delegation, the allocation of work amongst the staff and the role of the senior clerks. There was clear evidence that the level of delegation is not yet consistent across the Group.

Overall the potential value in the plethora of information now available was recognized. However, managers are not yet familiar enough with the information to put it to fully effective use. Moreover, some cynical views emerged. In particular, one manager referred to the available information as 'vast, duplicated, incomprehensible'. The manager is swamped. There is a need for more targeted and therefore selective information. It is interesting to note that managers had little or no information, other than impressions, on what their competitors were doing. Not all branch managers could give a clear idea of which competitor controlled the largest market share locally. (A first one-day workshop on the Management Information System was held during the final week of interviewing.)

Key success factors

Managers were asked to indicate what factors would be considered when the performance of their department or branch was being assessed and what the key success factors were for the Group as a whole. Table 6.1 sets out the answers given to the question on assessment. The answers were given unprompted and, as would be expected, financial issues predominate. Interestingly, customer care and staff-related criteria emerge as well. Some managers suggested that they were unsure how the department was assessed. The process was seen by some to comprise too subjective a selection of the performance figures. Conflicting targets were imposed by sales, quality control and operations departments. More than one manager seemed concerned about the priority given to various targets. 'Is sales our salvation?' said one. Can we be successful if we 'force feed sales down customers throats' said another.

Lack of clarity in the group structure has caused a perception

Table 6.1 Performance Assessment

Criterion	Frequency of response
Sales volume	23
Profit	22
Costs	14
Bad debts/quality of lending	8
Customer care/complaints	7
Fee income	6
Staff development	6
Motivation of staff	5
Image of branch/bank	4
Absenteeism/turnover of staff	2
Good audit reports	1
Dormancy	1

amongst many managers of a conflict between audit and sales. Managers recognized that there would always be a balance to draw between the intention to increase sales and the need to ensure high quality lending and control. However managers clearly perceived contradictory 'signals' from the functional managers concerned. There appeared to be problems of communication from the group management team to branch managers in this regard. Several managers felt that there was unnecessary overlap between quality control and audit at both branch and, sometimes, at regional level. That said, managers felt that quality control was a valid function that had led to a significant reduction in bad debts. Nevertheless quality control was often unable to add anything to the notes obtained by the lending manager. This suggests that quality control should be utilized only in certain circumstances (i.e. at the request of the lending manager, for certain sizes or types of facility, as a random check, or for new business).

When asked to give the key success factors, managers mentioned different issues. Many were clear that the image and product offering of Money Matters, both locally and nationally, was important. Building team spirit was also seen as vital. Branch managers clearly wondered whether they had the right mix of skills in their own teams. One made the point that while he was now

responsible for recruitment he had no training in selection interviewing. Linked to this, many managers questioned whether
Money Matters was getting the right staff to deal with the
increased emphasis on selling. Communication was thought to be
good now although managers seemed universally to feel that there
were too many meetings, they were poorly structured and sometimes boring and frustrating. Here managers were referring to all
meetings which took staff or branch managers away from the
branch, including training. Some managers thought the quality of
staff was good and their loyalty excellent. Much more training was
now being carried out but some thought this was too much. There
were problems in obtaining relief staff to cover for staff away
training, but even greater problems for the staff attempting to
absorb the training and put it into practice. Despite the increased
training, several branch managers saw gaps in the technical knowledge of their staff.

Branch managers felt that there needs to be greater lending
authority at branch level. Customer service and account relationships would thereby improve. This was currently being reviewed
but several doubted that any changes made would be sufficient.
However, the group concept was seen to be working and some
managers felt that a period of stability was now needed.

Money Matters is adapting a new style in branch design developed by a leading design consultant. New-style branches, new-
style accounts and a new style of banking generally were all seen as
most important. But throughout the interviews many expressed
doubts. The products were too complex. The staff were not
properly trained. There was a lack of information. 'We have
always been selling – it's no real change.' One is forced to
conclude that many of those interviewed see change as inevitable,
but also feel somewhat overwhelmed. They evince lack of information, understanding and control. Most importantly, they evince
powerful loyalty to the company which for some is of little help. Is
Money Matters depending over much on the loyalty of its staff,
they say?

One interviewee was very positive about the group plan. He felt
that all managers understood it. Moreover, it had been communicated to all staff. The self-esteem and confidence of staff at all
levels was needed. He felt that senior managers need to spend

more time in branches communicating with staff. Yet the majority of those interviewed made no mention of the group plan. (The sales manager was in the process of visiting all branches to present the group plan to staff during the period of the interviews.)

Customer service and branch image drew many mentions as key success factors. Premises needed to be inviting and staff positive in their approach to customers. A positive team effort was needed to achieve all of this. Too much job segmentation was not helpful and flexibility was needed. Some branch managers clearly felt that flexibility could be improved, albeit this was not the case in the smaller branches (as might be expected). There is nothing to stop branch managers re-allocating tasks within a branch, and some clearly do operate more flexibly than others. Lack of staff training in banking operations was one reason offered to explain why some managers operate their branches less flexibly than others. People also needed to be able to see achievable targets. Some targets were demotivating. More than one manager felt that branch managers and account managers were not active enough in pursuing/developing new business. Everyone was 'bogged down in reams of paper'. Better information, systems, premises and people might help, but one is still left with the basic fact that attitude changes are needed if the move to a sales culture is to be achieved.

Strengths, weaknesses and actions for improvement

Unprompted responses to questions concerning strengths, weaknesses and actions for improvement are set out in Tables 6.2 and 6.3. These tables powerfully reinforce the analysis made thus far. Perhaps the most telling observation is that when asked to discuss the opportunities for improvement managers referred (very properly) to streamlining of systems and training, but not to the broader changes in the company culture which are now under way. Indeed, many references to the switch to the sales culture referred to this change in negative ways – 'the staff don't sell', 'these people did not join the bank to sell', and so on. This should surprise no one. Managers and staff are being asked to embrace very profound changes, very quickly.

Table 6.2 sets out the answers given in response to questions concerning the strengths and weaknesses of the company and opportunities for improvement and constraints within the

Table 6.2 Strengths, weaknesses, opportunities and constraints of Midvale Group

Strengths	Frequency of response	Weaknesses	Frequency of response
Loyalty and experience of staff	17	Quality of management calibre, selection, lack of praise to staff, co-ordination at group level of performance, distant from customers)	24
Area management team	13		
Customer service, speed of response	12		
Open style of management	9	Premises	10
Product range	5	Lack of delegation	9
Branch position	5	Operational (split sites, local representative, high national admin. costs, complex products)	9
Team spirit	3		
Customer base	2		
Growth in local economy	1		
		Poor on-the-job training	8
		Risk-averse culture	8
		Authorities too small	5
		Image (dealing with complaints)	5
		Systems problems	4

Opportunities	Frequency of response	Constraints	Frequency of response
Streamlining systems (returns, QC & Audit)	9	Under-staffed, resource limitations, reactive management, pressure	14
Operational improvements (service centre, technology)	4	Too much paper	7
Training courses available	2	Change (impact on jobs, staff, 'too fast' cynicism	6
		Returns	6
		Competition	6
		Too many meetings	3
		Lack of freedom to manage	2

company's structure. Table 6.3 lists ideas for improvement put forward by the managers.

In concluding this section it is worth emphasizing that the group has important strengths and the ability to perform amidst major

Table 6.3 Practical steps to improve efficiency and customer service (suggestions from managers interviewed)

Communication

More open management throughout the group
More staff meetings
Meetings with other branches and group
Meetings of senior clerks
Improved communication

Support

Improved performance feedback
Stress counselling
More support for staff during change
Improved support for account managers

Customer service/premises

More effective product briefing and training
Space
Premises and equipment
Counsellors/receptionists
Staff accessibility to customers
Layout of branches, open plan

Efficiency

Streamlined systems
Standing orders system
Diary-watch system
Improved delegation to clerical staff at group office
Staff development standards
Co-ordinate training
Job rotation for branch managers
Improved market information

---

changes. Managers demonstrated loyalty and commitment to the company and, in the main, strong motivation to improve performance. The problems and concerns identified are only to be expected when changes are under way. There is a recognition that the progress already made can be built upon to achieve improved performance in the future.

The Group has important strengths in its area management

team, its open style of management and, in particular, its staff. However, amongst its perceived weaknesses is the quality of management. Here the focus of the managers seemed to be at middle levels of management, both at group and branch level. Lack of coordination at group level referred mostly to the coordination of training, meetings and returns. All lead to much frustration and pressure at branch level. More important, perhaps, is the combination of a risk averse culture with concerns over the rate of current change. Many of the managers interviewed recognized that profound changes were under way but appeared to feel that they lacked any real control over change. Several referred to the cynicism that can emerge. They felt that too many managers at all levels in Money Matters were 'rule bound'. Everyone seemed more concerned to cover their own position than take risks. This had a profound effect on the lower levels of staff. The managers interviewed clearly felt that the risk-averse culture makes it difficult to achieve changes in training and some were cynical about the prospects for change in general.

STAFF ATTITUDE SURVEY

The organizational diagnosis questionnaire set out in Part I of the workbook (see p. 21) was distributed to all staff in the Midvale Group (approximately 300 in all). Participation in this survey was anonymous and entirely voluntary. Staff were asked to complete the questionnaire and return it in a plain, sealed envelope to the group office, via their own branch manager. Responses were received from 208 staff members (60 per cent response).

The results of the survey suggest a considerable measure of weakness. Using the criteria set out in Rule 2 of the questionnaire analysis (see p. 25), twelve out of forty statements reveal areas of potential weakness. Applying Rule 3 to the responses, twelve out of forty statements reveal areas of weaknesses. One point should be made at once. The group, the region and Money Matters as a whole have been going through dramatic changes in the last few years. The organization is currently in the midst of a series of profound changes, in technology, working procedures, culture and management. In consequence many people feel, and are, under great pressure. This is reflected in these results.

Listed below are the ten statements which are identified as potential weaknesses by applying Rules 2 and 3.

4   I am encouraged to develop my full potential.
12   The salary that I receive is commensurate with the job that I perform.
18   The way in which work tasks are divided is sensible and clear.
21   This organization sets realistic plans.
28   Encouragement and recognition is given for all jobs and tasks in this organization.
30   This organization's management team provides effective and inspiring leadership.
32   The work we do is always necessary and effective.
34   The way the work structure in this organization is arranged produces general satisfaction.
35   Conflicts of view are resolved by solutions which are understood and accepted.
38   My boss's management stule helps me in the performance of my own work.

Two more statements emerge as identified weaknesses from Rule 2.

13   I have all the information and resources I need to do a good job.
17   I feel motivated by the work I do.

These twelve statements deal with three key areas: management style; support; and the organization of work. Responses to statements 4, 28, 30, 35 and 38 suggest that staff perceive a lack of encouragement, recognition, help, leadership and satisfactory decision-making from management. Responses to statements 21 and 13 suggest that staff do not perceive realistic plans nor do they feel adequately informed or resourced. This raises a key question of whether staff believe the company's present position and future plans to be credible. Responses to statements 12, 18, 32, 34 and 17 indicate that staff do not feel that work is effectively structured, is always necessary and is motivating.

In many respects these results suggest that there has not yet been fullyeffective communication from the group team to branches. Many of these weaknesses ought not to be so prevalent if the group concept were working more effectively. Allowing for the full benefit of the impact of changes on these results it must be emphasized that these data raise serious questions about how far and how fast Money Matters can achieve change without devoting more attention to managing the implementation of change with all its attendant pressures.

We turn now to the areas for improvement identified by staff. Here we deal with the questions listed in the organizational improvement analysis (see p. 28), and some additional questions that were included to 'tailor' that technique to meet the needs of Money Matters plc. The questionnaire asks what prevents the department or branch from being better at its function. The responses of the staff are listed in Table 6.4. Facilities, training, work pressure, ineffective management and information all feature and, of these, work pressure and facilities attract the largest number of comments. This is consistent with the earlier results. It is worth noting that staff view training as inadequate, despite the recent increased activity in this area. However, the staff are referring mainly to what they see as a lack of training in bank systems, rather than training in general.

The responses to the question of what practical steps should be taken to improve efficiency are listed in Table 6.5. The organization of work attracts a large number of responses. More autonomy at the till refers to greater scope to deal with queries and complaints. In theory this is available but it appears that in the risk-averse culture some staff feel that they are not trusted to deal with queries. Some branch managers also said that staff lacked the necessary training. It must be said that under the pressure of a queue of customers till staff are instructed to refer complaints 'up the line'. Even so some frustration is evinced over this issue. However, it should be noted that training (particularly in-branch training) and information are also seen as important. Under-management staff asked for more decisive leadership, improved support (linked mostly to in-branch training) and recognition for good work.

Table 6.4 What prevents the department from being better at its function?

Response	Frequency of response

Work pressure
    Short-staffed
    Insufficient time
    Pressure
    Not enough personal attention
        for customers
    Others' mistakes
    Counter service inadequate
    Cost cutting
	75

Facilities
    Lack of space
    Poor facilities
    Poor premises
    Poor computers
	52

Ineffective management
    No leadership
    Poor attitude from manager
    No support
    Too much bureaucracy
    Inefficient organization of work
	33

Training
    Inadequate
    Lack of experience in branch
        systems and procedures
	24

Information
    Not enough information
    Too much paper
	13

When asked how relationships with other departments might be improved, staff referenced job rotation and improved team-working as important. The two are linked of course. Job rotation would increase contact and therefore help with team-working. Other suggestions for improving inter-departmental relationships are improved support from group/region and improved communication (e.g. quicker responses to queries). The full list of responses is given in Table 6.6.

Table 6.5 What practical steps should be taken to improve department efficiency?

Response	Frequency of response
Organization of work	75
Job descriptions/clarification	
Efficient organization of workflow	
More autonomy/authority for people at till	
Delegation	
Realistic targets	
Assign people to work for which they are suited	
Motivation, payment by results	
Improved training	49
Out-of-branch	
In-branch (22)	
Generally	
Information	48
More product information	
Improved communication (area and region)	
Less complicated information	
Facilities	36
Tills	
Computers	
Generally	
More staff	34
Management	17
Leadership	
Support	
Praise for good work	

The responses to the question of what practical steps should be taken to improve customer service included more staff and better facilities, as well as training in customer service (now under way). Information and management issues were also mentioned. The full list of responses is given in Table 6.7

Staff were asked to rate whether or not they were given, or had access to, enough information to do their job effectively. The results are as follows:

Table 6.6 What practical steps should be taken to improve relationships between your departments and other departments?

Response	*Frequency of response*
Better team-working	33
Job rotation Visits to other branches Rotation Greater contact between departments More knowledge of each other's jobs	32
Communication	17
Support from group/region Reduce remoteness Improve support on marketing Coordination of requests for information Less condescending requests for information	14
Organization of work Greater accuracy Keep relevant information together	12

Yes	38
Most of the time	80
Some of the time	66
No	18

The results suggest that staff are not entirely satisfied with the information available to them. When asked how information might be improved staff referred to the organization of information and to the use of meetings. Table 6.8 lists specific suggestions. Staff feel that information should be presented to them more selectively, although all information should be available. To this end they suggest that an index or even library service might be considered. More effective use of briefing meetings to inform staff about products is also needed and some is now under way.

Table 6.7 What practical steps should be taken to improve performance for your customers?

Response	Frequency of response
Facilities	47
Answerphone	
Computer terminals	
Enquiry counter	
Supply of product leaflets	
Viewdata	
More staff	44
More individual attention	
Training	32
Information	23
More information before product release	
More up-to-date information	
Management	21
More authority for cashiers to deal with problems	
More supportive management	
Managers to be available to see customers	
More decisive management	
Staff to feel confident about products	

Table 6.8 What practical steps should be taken to improve the information you receive?

Response	Frequency of response
Organization of information	88
Summaries	
Index	
Library	
Managers to pass on relevant information	
More fact-finders	
Meetings	24
More branch visits	
More regular briefings	
Key-time staff to attend meetings	
Brief staff before customers	
More relevant in-branch product training	

THE STAFF MEETINGS

Once the questionnaires were completed two meetings were held with representative groups of staff to provide the opportunity to discuss the results more fully. The discussions at these meetings powerfully reinforced the picture emerging from the question-naires. Further clarification was obtained on a number of points.

Training

The staff view is that the external training is good, but they are not always able to put it into practice. In-branch training is poor partly because of staffing levels. 'It has become more acceptable to make mistakes' was a point widely shared. Pressure on staff had led to increased overtime yet better training might enable junior staff to perform more effectively. More senior staff felt that job knowledge was often poor. Staff also felt that the external training concen-trated too much on what to do without advising on how to do it.

Impact of changes

There was a clear perception that staff views were not considered, that information was late and that circulars were often condes-cending in tone. Viewdata was one example of a system which 'arrived' with no preparation or training. Given existing workloads the staff opinion was that many of them might not sell a newly introduced account because of the additional paperwork that would create. Everyone was under pressure. One staff member felt that absenteeism had increased and that this was due to increased pressure.

The change to a sales culture was accepted, but staff questioned whether everyone was able to sell. Nevertheless, they recognized the problem of performance-related pay where job specialization arose. Attitudes here were somewhat cynical. The 'goal-posts' had moved on this scheme. More immediately there was general concern that not all branch managers treated staff in the same way.

An example was given of a staff member who regularly deputized but did not receive deputizing pay because the period involved was always four rather than the qualifying five days. Other branch managers treated their staff differently.

Work organization

There was a strong recognition that staff skills and experience were not being utilized sufficiently. In particular the senior clerks could do more, have more customer contact and be more involved in team-leading. Branch managers should delegate more. At least one was widely known to open the post and prepare duty lists and dormancy lists. In such a case the branch manager is less accessible to customers and customer service is poor. All staff felt the procedures could be simplified. Many felt that senior clerks should meet to discuss problems, perhaps all visiting the 'best-organized branch in the group' as a means of getting improvements throughout the group.

Management style

Management style was recognized as more human and less distant from people than in the past. People management was judged to have improved and this was helping morale. However, staff felt that managers underestimated them, did not provide clear or decisive leadership and did not listen. 'Who can you talk to?' 'What will it lead to?' were frequent questions.

CONCLUSIONS

The picture that has been portrayed is of a group in which managers and staff are undergoing very significant changes with many more expected. Staff are concerned that these changes are neither well-planned nor effectively managed. More fundamentally the attitude changes so important to creating a new sales and performance culture have not yet emerged, at least not consistently. This, however, is to be expected and to ignore that, or to criticize those who have not yet comes to terms with the new situation would be to reinforce the constraints which make those attitude changes difficult and time-consuming.

Dramatic changes can be confusing and uncomfortable. Four basic requirements are needed to help people subjected to change:

1   *Empathy*
They want people to listen to them, without judging them. The flow of communication must be both ways.

2   *Information*
They need to understand why the changes are needed, how they will work, what the impact on themselves will be, i.e. 'What am I trying to deal with?'

3   *Credibility*
They need to believe in the changes. They need to be convinced that they will work, will achieve objectives that make sense to them, will resolve problems they see as real. The group plan needs to be communicated effectively.

4   *Ideas for action*
They need suggestions for actions, options, plans. They want to put ideas into action, to try them out, to learn from experience. Many of the managers and staff are clear about what is required of them, but not how to achieve a new approach.

Here the evidence collected suggests that there is too much pressure and too much downward communication for many managers and staff to feel that they are listened to or to understand the changes in preparation (too much information, sometimes contradictory and often too late). This means that many do not believe in the changes. Moreover, if anything, the staff see some of the changes as at best irrelevant to the problems they perceive. Overall, whilst many people have ideas for improvement, there is a sense that so much is changing that perhaps it is better to leave things as they are at our level – to not sell a new account!

RECOMMENDATIONS

Using the guidelines set out in the Organizational Diagnosis and Implementation sections of Part I of this workbook what recommendation would you make? You should try to identify:

■ A list of specific recommended actions to deal with problems identified by the analysis of suggestions made by managers and staff.
■ Some more general recommendations designed to help the managers cope more effectively with the dramatic changes that are now being experienced in Money Matters.

Over the page the recommendations actually implemented are listed. Before turning the page you may find it an interesting exercise to list your own now.

Recommendations

a

b

c

d

e

Specific recommendations

(i) Review jobs and work organization at branch and departmental level. Ensure that delegation to staff is actively carried out.

(ii) Encourage branch managers to further develop in-branch training on systems and procedures.

(iii) Encourage branch managers to further develop new product briefing meetings with staff.

(iv) Review the role of senior clerks and branch managers regarding in-branch training, staff management, lending and customer contact.

(v) Examine the use of job rotation of branch managers, partly to encourage delegation, partly as a means of transferring ideas between branches.

(vi) Increase contact between staff. Examine the use of regular meetings of senior clerks to review branch problems (a senior clerk's review group) and to identify areas for improvement.

(vii) Encourage managers to provide positive feedback to staff.

(viii) Group management and branch management to communicate the group plan throughout the organization.

(ix) Clarify and agree a common branch/departmental performance assessment framework based upon the existing systems.

(x) Ensure greater coordination at group level of meetings, training and requests for returns. Place the onus of responsibility for justifying returns to the staff concerned on the manager asking for them.

(xi) Review the role of quality control.

(xii) Review the presentation of information to managers and staff including the use of indexing and other means of selective provision.

(xiii) Review the approach to meetings, reduce the length of presentations and include focused workshop activity where managers can work on group problems and issues.

(xiv) Stress counselling should be available to help managers and others cope with the pressure of change. One or more managers should be trained in the essentials of stress counselling with a clear brief to provide help and/or to refer people on to a more professional source of help should that be needed.

STRATEGY FOR CHANGE: MONEY MATTERS PLC

We have now analysed change at the Midvale Group of Money Matters plc. What do the analysis and recommendations tell us about the need for a national strategy to manage the changes that are being experienced throughout the company? Using the project management strategy for managing change, outlined in Chapter 5, try to identify the key elements for a change strategy under the following six headings:

■ Management structure to implement change
■ Planning for implementation
■ Leadership
■ Long-term criteria in change planning and implementation
■ Flexible controls
■ Communications plan

Use the discussion of Money Matters given in the various stages of Part I of this book as you do so.

7 Agenda for implementing change

We complete this workbook by identifying an agenda for change. Following the agenda brings no guarantees of success but should increase its likelihood. The main ingredients of successful change programmes are:

1 A clear strategic aim is needed for implementation. The benefits of change are often slow to be achieved and intangible. Unfortunately the costs are often more tangible and are certainly more immediate. Therefore people need to understand why the changes are being made. What competitive advantage will the organization achieve if the changes are successfully implemented? I remember working hundreds of hours of overtime trying to get an electronically controlled crane working effectively in 1961. Why? The contract under which it was being built had a penalty clause against late delivery. Much more important however was the customer.

It was a company which was one of those who launched the 'container revolution' in the 1960s. The factory manager had made it clear to us that success now meant major sales in the future. We responded!

2 *Support* at top level is crucial to success. Senior managers must be clearly *accountable* for change. New systems, new product launches and new structures are expensive and disruptive. It is important that senior managers are clearly accountable so that people can see how expenditure and progress is being controlled. Increasingly, organizations now adopt a *project management* approach to reinforce this accountability.

3 Major changes often lead to changes in the power structure of the organization. This is another reason why successful implementation needs project management with the involvement of users and line managers.

4 Implementation must be carefully planned and managed. It will take time and have far-reaching effects. *Achieving ownership* is crucial. Managing the stress induced by change, helping people to cope with change and understanding its impact are all important.

5 Where possible changes should be designed to depend on existing systems, procedures, cultures and traditions. Ensuring *maximum compatibility* creates a better basis for implementation.

6 The main problems to be solved in implementation are *cross-functional* problems.

7 The pace of change needs careful planning. Longer planning leads to quicker implementation, early success and faster diffusion.

8 Pragmatism, rather than a technology-driven 'big project' approach is more likely to deliver success. 'The excellent is the enemy of the good' is a relevant saying. People respond to pragmatism. They respond if the planned changes appear to deal with problems they recognize.

9 Systems should be built in to reward relevant behaviour. Providing early feedback of success helps. Developing reward systems to reinforce change is another powerful means of supporting implementation.

10 The importance of role modelling should not be ignored. Changing your behaviour to provide an example may be needed.

11 Appropriate training and support systems need to be established. However, provide flexibility and allow users control over training. Too little and over-rigid training can be a hindrance. Training provided before people have accepted change will be of little value.

8 Change and the person

As I have emphasized throughout this book the topic of managing change cannot be seen as a mechanistic activity. Managers can draw as many neat boxes as they wish on planning charts but the real barriers are within the individual's perceptions, skills and capacity to tolerate ambiguity. We conclude this book by reflecting on the impact of change on the individual. In particular, we will examine the phases of adaption to change. Effective change leaders understand the way that individuals react to change and use the principles described in this chapter to ease the process.

CHANGE AND STRESS

Change creates anxiety, uncertainty and stress, even for those managing change. Even people who are fully committed to change may experience stress. Seldom are there any guarantees that the new approach will work, that it will deliver the goods. Those who want the change to be successful often find themselves working long hours, dealing with problems, trying to overcome the doubts of others, and doing everything necessary to see the changes through. In working life change and role strain are two sources of stress. Role strain can be caused by a number of factors: not being involved in decision-making, having inadequate managerial support, having to cope with technological or other changes, having to maintain standards of performance even under difficult circumstances, having responsibility for people who are uncooperative. All these are likely to occur in a period of change! In life outside work moving home is a key source of stress and this sometimes flows from change. Thus we should not be surprised by the links between change and stress.

One simple and helpful idea for managers dealing with change involves looking at the relationship between self-esteem, perform-ance and stress. This is shown in Figure 8.1. The relationship turns out to be curvi-linear both for performance and self-esteem. The relationship is well established. The problem is that people are different. We don't all fit neatly onto one curve. However the general nature of the relationship seems to hold. In any event if change causes stress we cannot be at the left-hand end of the curve. We must be moving in the direction shown in Figure 8.2 and therefore on the downward slope of the curve. Is there a threshold beyond which behaviour becomes volatile and unpre-dictable? In fact people respond differently. Some stress motivates people by providing a challenge. However, we need to avoid stressing ourselves and others too much. This can leave to people feeling swamped and to middle managers reverting to more auto-cratic management styles.

COPING WITH MAJOR ORGANIZATIONAL CHANGE

So much for change and stress. But what happens if we look at the impact of change over time? This section will consider the impact

Figure 8.1 Relationship between performance/self-esteem and stress

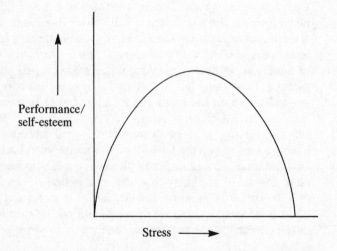

Figure 8.2 Thresholds for performance/self-esteem in periods of stress

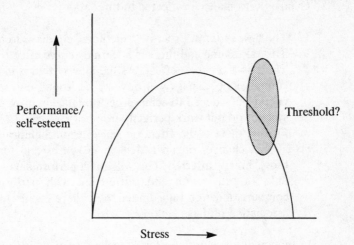

of change upon the people directly affected, which often includes many middle and senior managers. The concern here is with the people who must take on new tasks, develop new skills, or are transferred, regraded or retrained. Once changes emerge people must learn to cope as individuals. A simple model will be used to describe how people experience change and then consider how they can cope with the pressures created by change. Understanding this can allow senior managers to provide practical support for people undergoing change and may better enable them to avoid creating constraints on people which make their personal task of coping all the harder.

Often the problems of implementing change are classed as 'resistance to change'. In fact the change situation is more complex than this phrase suggests and capable of a more constructive interpretation. Managers often encourage 'resistance to change' by dealing with people as if that is the response they expect. Here the practical and positive steps which can be taken to support people as they cope with change are considered.

Change creates uncertainty, anxiety and stress. Moreover, changes which have a large impact on the work that people do will affect their self-esteem. This is well established through the research of Cooper (1981) and Miller and de Vries (1985). Linked to the impact on self-esteem is a performance effect. In periods of change performance is affected in three ways:

1 The new systems, processes, methods, etc. have to be learned. This takes time and there is a learning curve effect.
2 There is a progress effect. As the new system is installed and commissioned, snags will have to be ironed out and modifications introduced to achieve performance improvement. New systems do not work perfectly from the outset.
3 Finally, there is the effect on self-esteem. Significant organizational changes create a decline in self-esteem for many of those directly affected. This will affect performance. Whilst the links of satisfaction and self-esteem with performance are complex and not fully understood there seems to be some association of these factors.

In practice performance will decline once major changes are under way as result of a combination of these factors. In a period of change, attempts to rebuild self-esteem become the main driving force to achieve higher performance. This can be helped by action on the learning curve and progress fronts: the coping cycle. The model shown in Figure 8.3 consists of five stages. These are

Figure 8.3 The coping cycle

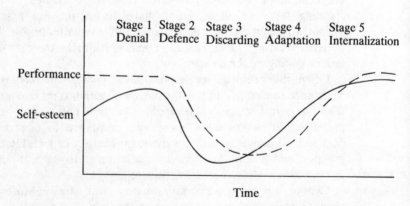

Absolute levels are unimportant, only relative levels are meaningful. Problems of measurement are significant but do not obscure the assessment of relative levels of performance or self-esteem.

capable of more detailed analysis but for the present purposes this simplified form is sufficient. The model is taken, in particular, from the work of Adams, Hayes and Hopson (1976) on coping with personal life changes.

Stage 1: denial

'We have always done things this way!' 'Why change, we are making a profit, aren't we?' 'Don't change a winning team'. These are some of the ways denial can find expression. Faced with the possibility of change people will often find value in their present circumstances, often in work situations which they have complained of previously. This apparent paradox should not be surprising. People are impelled by contradictory motivations. Coal miners threatened with the closure of a pit will defend their pit and jobs with some vigour, yet still believe fervently that working conditions are arduous and even dangerous.

If major organizational changes come suddenly and dramatically then a kind of paralysis can often occur. People seem overwhelmed, unable to plan or even understand what is going on. Often there is a longish period of gestation as ideas are discussed and concrete changes planned. Even if these changes are not particularly new or dramatic this paralysis may be felt just as intensely. However, the tendency to deny new ideas, at least at first, does seem to be a fairly general reaction. The advantages of the present situation become emphasized and attachments to the job, the work-group and the existing skills are recognized. Thus it is that self-esteem can increase, particularly if the presence of an external threat leads to increased group cohesion. If self-esteem does increase performance is unlikely to improve, either because the discussion of impending change can absorb energy or because there are systems in place which may hold back performance improvement, e.g. payment systems. If the change is dramatic, novel and traumatic, involving, say, a sudden job change or redundancy, then this stage can involve an immediate decline in performance. Generally, however, there is a warning period and performance will not decline immediately. One way individuals respond at this stage is to 'minimise' the impact of change. This allows people time to face up to a few realities.

Stage 2: defence

In time reality arrives. The early discussion of changes leads to concrete plans and programmes of change. Now the realities of change become clearer and people must begin to face new tasks: working for a new boss, or with a different group of people, perhaps in a different department or a new location. Thus they become aware that they must come to terms with the way they work, and perhaps more general changes in life, if, for example, relocation is required. This can lead to feelings of depression and frustration because it can be difficult to work out how to deal with these changes. This stage is often characterized by defensive behaviour. People may attempt to defend their own job, their own territory. Often this will be articulated as ritualistic behaviour. I can remember the introduction of computer-aided learning in business schools many years ago. Many people embraced these developments enthusiastically. Some simply rejected them: 'my subject is unsuitable'. One colleague provided an impressive show of activity on the computer, finally concluding that after much effort he had failed to make computer-aided learning work for his subject. Years later computer-aided learning in that subject is commonplace. Was this a ritual? Again, this defensive behaviour seems to have the effect of creating time and 'space' to allow people to come to terms with changes.

Stage 3: discarding

There now emerges a process of discarding. The previous stages have focused powerfully upon the past. Now people begin to let go of the past and look forward to the future. We do not know how this happens. We know that support can be helpful, as can providing people with the opportunity to experiment with new systems without the pressure of formal training programmes, and so on. Now it is possible for optimistic feelings to emerge. It may well be that the discarding process is impelled by an awakening sense that the present anxieties are too much to bear, or that perhaps the future is not as forbidding as it first seemed. Behaviour may be observed which appears to identify the individuals with the changes involved. They will start to talk openly and constructively about the new system. They will ask questions about it. In a sense they will say 'Well, here it is, we are committed to it, here's how I see it'. People may begin to solve problems, take the initiative and recipient will, in order to communicate, but if they pass on the information they have, they usually do so without attempting to make it intelligible.

EFFECTIVE IMPLEMENTATION OF CHANGE

Some guidelines for the effective implementation of change can now be outlined. Managing change requires us to:

1   Provide people with help to deal with change, recognizing the valued skills that they may now no longer use, and encourage them to see the future benefits of change, where this is appropriate.
2   Avoid over-organizing so that there is flexibility to deal with problems. New systems are never 100 per cent successful straightaway. Managers need the flexibility to allow adaptation along the way.
3   Communicate, communicate, always communicate! Effective communication is crucial but this means quality, not quantity, of communication. Check the quality of communication via feedback from staff.
4   Recognize that the problems others experience are real problems. Empathize. Don't ignore them, face up to them.
5   Gain full commitment to change by supporting people. Reward them, provide positive feedback and involve them at an early stage.

All of this requires a more systematic and sensitive approach to how change is planned and managed, an approach that is sensitive to the needs of people and sensitive to the problems and opportunities of the business. We hope this book has provided you with some techniques to help you approach change management in this way.

REFERENCES

Adams, J., Hayes, J. and Hopson, B (1976) *Transitions – Understanding and Managing Personal Change*, Oxford: Martin Robertson.

even demonstrate some leadership. Thus self-esteem begins to improve.

Discarding is initially a process of perception. People come to see that the change is both inevitable and/or necessary. Adaptation starts with recognition. Here we see human courage in difficult circumstances as the individual accepts new 'realities'. This can be exciting for individuals and groups. In taking the risk of publicly facing a new reality, there is a sense in which they reestablish their own identity; the identity which may have seemed threatened by the changes being introduced.

The crisis of change creates great tensions within the people involved. These provide many reasons for people to feel upset and disorientated: a new job appears to be of lesser status than the old one; valued skills seem unnecesary; the new work seems frustrating; the new system appears to be unusual, even frightening, although with practice it becomes commonplace. The crucial point is that this process needs time. Discarding involves experimentation and risk. Time is needed for individuals to recreate their own sense of identity and self-esteem as they 'grow' into the new situation.

Stage 4: adaptation

Now a process of mutual adaptation emerges. Rarely do new systems, procedures, structures or machines work effectively first time. Individuals begin to test the new situation and themselves, trying out new behaviours, working to different standards, working out ways of coping with the changes. Thus the individual learns. Other individuals also adapt. Fellow workers, supervisors and managers all learn as the new system is tried out. Finally, technical and operational problems are identified and modifications made to solve them. Thus progress is made.

Significant amounts of energy are involved during this stage. Often the process of trial and error, of effort and setback, and the slow building of performance can be a source of real frustration. In these circumstances people can appear angry. This is not resistance to change, rather it is the natural consequence of trying to make a new system work, experiencing partial or complete failure, which may or may not be under the control of the individuals concerned. This anger is not evidence of attempts to oppose but rather it articulates the feelings of those trying to make the new system work. Whilst managers should ensure the right training and support is available, they should generally remain in the background, allowing the people directly involved to make the new system work. By doing so these people will develop the skills, understanding and attachments needed for the system to be run effectively in the longer term.

Stage 5: internalization

The people involved have created a new system, process and organization. New relationships between people and processes have been tried, modified and accepted. These have become incorporated into the understanding of the new work situation. This is a cognitive process through which people make sense of what has happened. Now the new behaviour becomes part of 'normal' behaviour.

It seems that people experience change in these ways, initially as disturbance, perhaps even as a shock, then come to accept its reality, testing it out and engaging in a process of mutual adaptation and finally, they come to terms with it. Self-esteem and performance vary, during the process initially declining, and then growing again. The variation in performance flows from mutually reinforcing individual and operational causes, as has been observed. The 'engine' for rebuilding performance is the self-esteem of the people involved.

It is not suggested that people go through these stages neatly, nor that all go through them at the same time, or at the same rate. Some may not go beyond the denial of change. The important point is that people do seem to experience significant changes in these ways and this leads us to a number of practical ways in which the problems of coping can be handled. Coping with the process of change places demands on the individuals involved. Various issues need to be faced either by the individuals or by managers. Note, however, that these issues are of concern to all affected by an organizational change, including managers.

REBUILDING SELF-ESTEEM

The ground covered in this section is summarized in Figure 8.4. In simple terms, it is suggested that individuals have four main categories of need which are required if they are to rebuild their

Figure 8.4 Rebuilding self-esteem

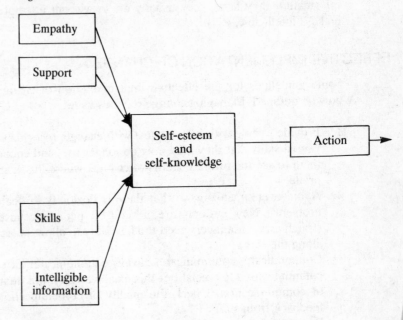

self-esteem during a programme of organizational change. They need intelligible information. They will probably need to develop new skills, even if only the skill of dealing with new people as colleagues or supervisors. They will need support to help them deal with the problems and encouragement to try out new systems. Provision of short workshops planned to achieve part or all of the work discussed in the preceding section can help. Technical support to solve problems is often needed. Access to people who can help is useful. Control over the rate of personal learning should be possible. All of these things can help, but most of all people need to be treated with empathy. First and foremost empathy is the main factor.

Understanding is a key issue. The skill of empathy is the struggle to understand. People can never fully see a situation others see it but they can struggle to try, and individuals will respond to that struggle. They will also respond adversely someone who clearly does not try. Making information intelligible to its recipient requires skill. People need to try to see things as

Cooper, G. (1981) *Psychology and Management*, London: Macmillan.

Miller, D. and de Vries, K. (1985) *The Neurotic Organization*, New York: Jossey-Bass.